Google Classroom:

2020 User Manual to Learn Everything You Need to Know to Use Google Classroom Effectively.

Google Classroom

Copyright © 2020

All rights reserved.

ISBN: 9798640468342

CONTENTS

Introduction 4

Chapter 1 – Benefits of Google Classroom for Everyone 6

Chapter 2 – Getting Started with Google Classroom 19

Chapter 3 – How to Create and Manage a Class 30

Chapter 4 – How to Set Due Dates, Manage Homework and Assignments 46

Chapter 5 – Inviting Students and Teachers to Classes 57

Chapter 6 – How to Grade Assignments and Then Put Them on Google sheets 68

Chapter 7 – How to Motivate Pupils 79

Chapter 8 – The Best Google Classroom Extensions 91

Chapter 9 – Top Five Hidden Features of Google Classroom 101

Chapter 10 – Top Useful Apps for Google Classroom 109

Conclusion 130

Introduction

Google Classroom is an excellent web service that came into existence for schools by Google with the focus on building, assigning and accessing assignments digitally (a great way to eradicate the use of paper). The main reason for creating the classroom is to increase the speed and ease transferring files between students and teachers in a school. The Classroom merges with Google Drive to create and assign assignments, Google Sheets, Docs and Slides for the act of writing, for exchanging of information it utilizes Gmail, and for organizing it utilizes the Calendar for Google. You can easily summon students to connect to a class using a secret code, or imported through a school domain. Every class builds an independent folder in each user's Drive, where the teacher grades work submitted by the student. Teachers can observe and check the progression for each student and then grade them, and teachers also have the option to leave comments or remarks.

Chapter 1 – Benefits of Google Classroom for Everyone

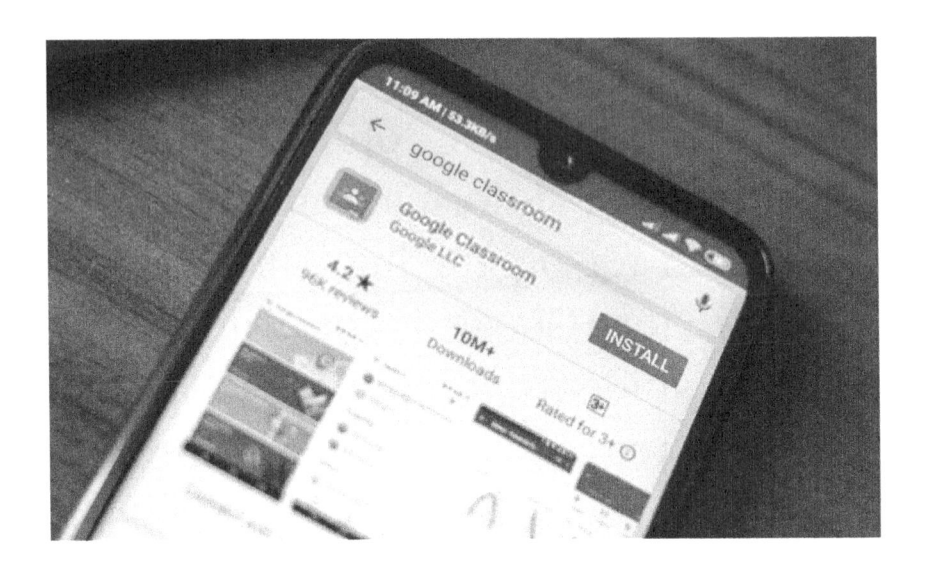

The tool has lots of benefits and is useful for college students and teachers as well as designers. Over the years, there has been increasing support for paperless classrooms in lots of universities and rural areas because it gives users the ability to complete lots of assignments and homework online.

The tool is easy and straightforward for students to utilize and more importantly minimizes the use of paper for users without classrooms who instead, attend virtual classes. The free platform consists of different advantages that include:

Platform is straightforward to use

It is easy to utilize and has a straightforward interface which is one of its best benefits. It provides guides to follow on each step while you use the platform, and when you get to its main page, it will invite you to interact with your class. Users can also create announcements and send them out to class members or teachers in your own time as well as give replies to notes from fellow students. Users do not require any special training or experience to utilize the platform, its software or interface.

Blend the platform with Google products

Users can easily integrate the platform with Google slides, sheets and docs. It provides a platform that syncs up with different free to use tools for an institution that runs on a tight budget. It also offers students and schools different ways to work in an advanced technology environment without purchasing any classroom software, which can be an expensive option.

Lecturers can now give several tasks to the students through the platform, and when students complete the project, they can check it off easily. The tool has excellent steps to follow to complete different tasks and ensures that it stays organized to avoid confusion at a later date.

Learning online

Over the years, there have been lots of institutions that require students to conduct online classes before students complete their degree. If your course in school for a Master's educational level has anything to do with education, there will be lots of tasks to perform online. To avoid confusion, teachers can also sign in as a student and go through the tasks so they can help first-timers learn it. Students can also take a course or upload contents into the internet world as well as learn several other things. The manufacturer created the platform to give users lots of exposure at a very young age.

Access to different materials

The internet is the place where you will find virtually everything and the platform allows students access to different types of materials. The need to have worksheets for projects is a thing of the past, and students can easily gain access to classroom materials without being present in school. It saves everyone lots of time and stress.

Differentiation

The tool is an excellent platform when it comes to differentiation because users can create different classes for one unit. It gives the teachers access to students privately in cases of correction, without any embarrassment. It also helps users create homework and assign them to students individually. The teacher can assign different tasks for students in a unit. You can also create different groups for students and fix each into where they can perform better. The platform is safe and flexible enough to use and ensure each student understands the requirements. Users can also modify groups, and they can recreate or delete classes.

Less paper

The platform took care of paper dependence for projects and users do not need paper because they now perform all of the tasks online. Students now require an only internet connection, and they can attend classes and perform several tasks. It also saves time and money.

Students interaction

One major benefit of the platform is the creation of different types of assignments which can include questions. You can also determine the points of each question and allow interaction among students. It creates rooms for learning among students, and everybody can learn from each other. Everyone can talk to one another and teachers can give direct instructions to students both generally and individually, and even with parents through the individual feedback, comments or email.

Give video lectures

One of the easiest platforms to perform that task is YouTube, and the classroom gives users the ability to attach a video they created to explain anything and then upload the embedded code of the content through URL. The platform comes with the video attribute and lets users make video lessons and create a competitive environment for students to learn. It is also a great rival to other video uploading platforms that come at a price because it comes with no price tag at all. Users can also include videos and differentiate their topics and sections.

Time-saving

Users can access all of the classroom resources in one location and students do not need to go to school to submit assignments. There is no need for a notebook because all of the lessons are now online, students can reply to questions and submit projects and homework on the platform. It also ensures that all of the projects and tasks remain organized, and users do not have to spend lots of time searching for projects or lost materials. It also makes the work of teachers easy because every student data, grades and assignment submission will be in one location, and that can save the teacher lots of valuable time.

Create accounts for new students

The classroom makes it very easy to add new students. Proceed to people tag, and you will find a teacher's list and students having a small person logo together with a plus sign. Select the logo close to teachers to create a new teacher and distribute workloads or assign classes. Students can also get into your class if you give them access to the code that you will find beneath the list containing students.

Differentiate skill levels

If there is more than one level of skill inside a classroom, the platform can let you distinguish them by creating different classrooms as much as you want to. You can create a class and give it the desired name. Teachers can have more than two student groups utilizing the platform, and the first group can be for level three while the second group would be for third grade. Users can use the platform to create different classes and separate the groups from one another, and each can function at its own pace. Teachers can also see each student from different classes on the same dashboard and give instructions and also help students who need extra help on projects. Teachers can also monitor the students.

Minimize excuses

Students always come up with different excuses for not completing their tasks or assignments, but this platform can help the teacher curb that habit and ensure that students perform their tasks and assignments. The platform enables the student to work on assignments and submit them digitally, which means the student cannot use the excuse, "I lost the assignment papers" any more. It also lets the parents monitor the student's progress. Lots of institutions utilize the online learning option and allow their students to attend classes comfortably from home.

Chapter 2 – Getting Started with Google Classroom

The classroom is a free platform that gives teachers the ability to provide instructions for students as well as share files with one another. Teachers can assign tasks and assignments to students and also grade the assignments without printing or the use of books. It is also a platform where users can communicate with one another and a service where teachers can post different announcements, homework and emails to the student as well as the student's parent. The platform utilizes Google drive, which is a cloud-based program for sharing files. It gives teachers the ability to utilize different Google services such as docs, forms and lots more to create and keep students' information.

The platform ensures that teaching becomes more productive by making assignments digital and enhances interactions among users as well as teachers to students. Users can create a new class, give feedback, share tasks and see all of the data in one location. Lots of institutions and non-profit organizations utilize the platform for educational purposes with zero cost. Anyone with a Google profile can utilize the platform for free, which makes it available to a lot of people and institutions. You can also utilize the platform for business purposes.

Benefits

The classroom has lots of advantages for teachers as well as students, everyone and anyone can utilize the platform for different types of projects including online classes, assignments and online learning. The benefits of the classroom include:

Easy setup - The platform is simple and straightforward to set up and use. Users can create a new class and invite teachers and students. They can also perform several tasks on the classwork page, and distribute and assign assignments, materials, information and questions.

Eradicates paper and saves time - The platform eradicates the use of paper for assignments and allows you to create classes and share information and enable interaction between users. Teachers can talk to the students directly and also remain organized and ensure that all of the student information remains in one location. The process also saves users lots of time and energy.

Excellent organization - It ensures that all of the information and materials remain organized, and users can view homework through the class stream, to-do page and class calendar. You will also find the materials for the class inside the Google drive folders.

Feedback and improved interaction - Users can create a homework, begin interactions in class, distribute materials between one another and send announcements. Users can interact inside the stream for class or through email. It also gives teachers the ability to monitor students progress and see who needs additional help and who has completed the project and also provide grades for the assignments as well as feedback.

Easy functionality with basic apps - The platform functions properly with different types of applications such as calendar, forms, drive, Google docs and lots of the basic applications.

Secure and inexpensive - Lots of institutions utilize the platform as well as non-profits organizations. It comes with no adverts and will not utilize any information about the students or teacher for advertising.

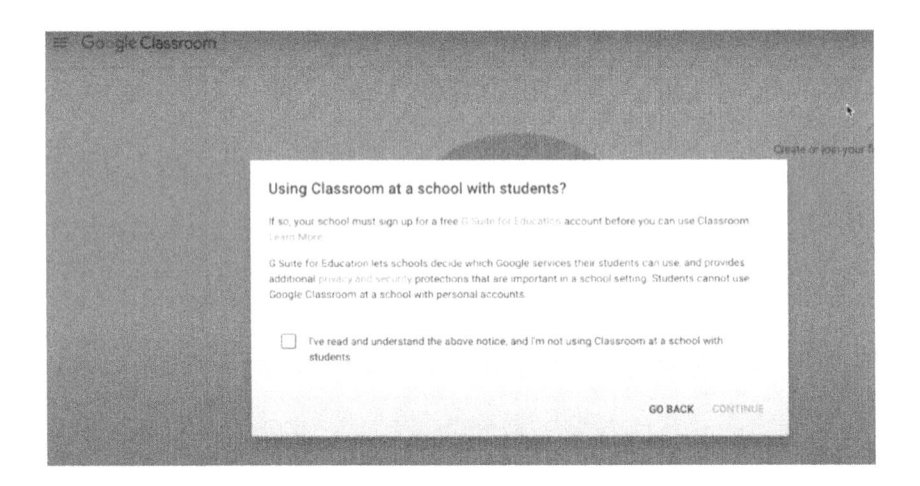

Accessing the platform

Before users start utilizing the platform, the first thing to do is to log into your Google account, and if you have no account, then you need to create one in order to utilize the classroom platform. You can access the platform via its official website, which is classroom.google.com. The platform also has a mobile application that users can download easily on Smartphones. It is one of the best applications for online classes and comfortable to utilize. The platform also ensures that different tasks are more convenient to perform, like creating and grading assignments on a personal computer. The platform allows teachers to create classes online where they can easily manage different student documents and materials as well as pass information. Teachers can also communicate with students in the same class individually and also as a group. The below steps will help you create a class when you are ready to begin:

Launch your web browser and proceed to the official platform website, which is classroom.google.com. Now log in, utilizing Google applications for education.

When you get to the welcome display, select the plus logo that you will find on top and create a class.

Now type the class section and name inside the dialogue box for creating classes.

Select create.

It will create your new class, and you will see the class with three major tabs.

Below are what the major tabs mean:

Stream: This is the location where users can make an announcement to the following users and also manage the homework assigned to a class. Users can create a new assignment and add different items as well as due dates. The platform will display upcoming homework on the left pane. If you are familiar with social media use, then you should know that the mode of message sending to an entire class is similar to the classroom platform. Users can exchange messages comfortably and even add attachments like videos and so on.

Students: It is the location where teachers can manage information and students in general. Teachers can send invitations to students in a class and control the level of permission given to the user. If you want to invite a user to a class, build a Google contact for the student within the application for education, and you should enable that the student is present in the institution's directory.

About: This is the location where users can add course definition and title, also include locations and additional items for the entire class folder inside the drive.

Create a new class: Users can create a new class by selecting the plus logo on the welcome display. You will find the sign close to the username section.

Give the class a new name or archive: On the welcome page, select the three dots that you will find close to the name of the class and you can either give the class a new name or archive it. Whenever you archive a class, it means that everyone can still access the file, but nobody can make any additional changes to that class because of the function that you performed on it. The class goes into its segment, and you should know that you can also reverse the action you performed and restore the class whenever you desire by viewing it. Select the dots and tap restore.

Access drive: Select the folder logo, and it will launch your drive, and you will find every classroom material in that section.

Chapter 3 – How to Create and Manage a Class

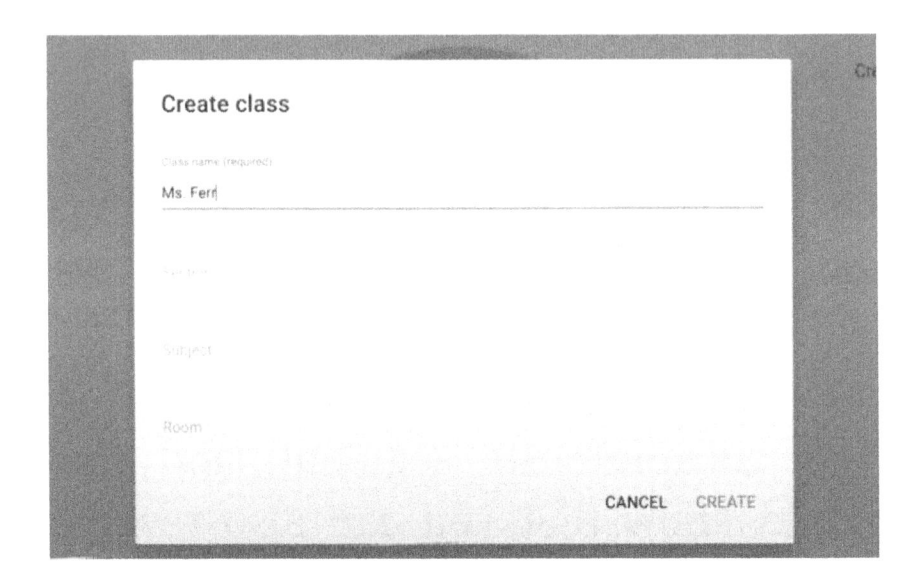

Over the past few years, there have been different types of research to support the utilization of users' partnerships and group works for assignments from class. The platform improves users' creativity in giving and assigning collective projects and offers several options to perform the task. The platform allows users to group assignments and teachers can also assign projects to students. You can perform the task of lesson assignment to a collection of students with simple steps, manage the class and unlock the possibilities that teachers and students could not utilize in the past.

Create group documents

The first thing is to create a document for the assignment. They include sheet, docs and so on and duplicate every group. Ensure that you add the name of the group or include a number at the end of the file name for easy identification and assistance. Users can store group assignments inside the drive where they can locate the stored document easily. It is also very easy to store documents in the folder of the classroom.

Create a topic for group assignment

Proceed to the tab of the class, click on the create button and select the topic. Find a suitable name for the project and input it, then save.

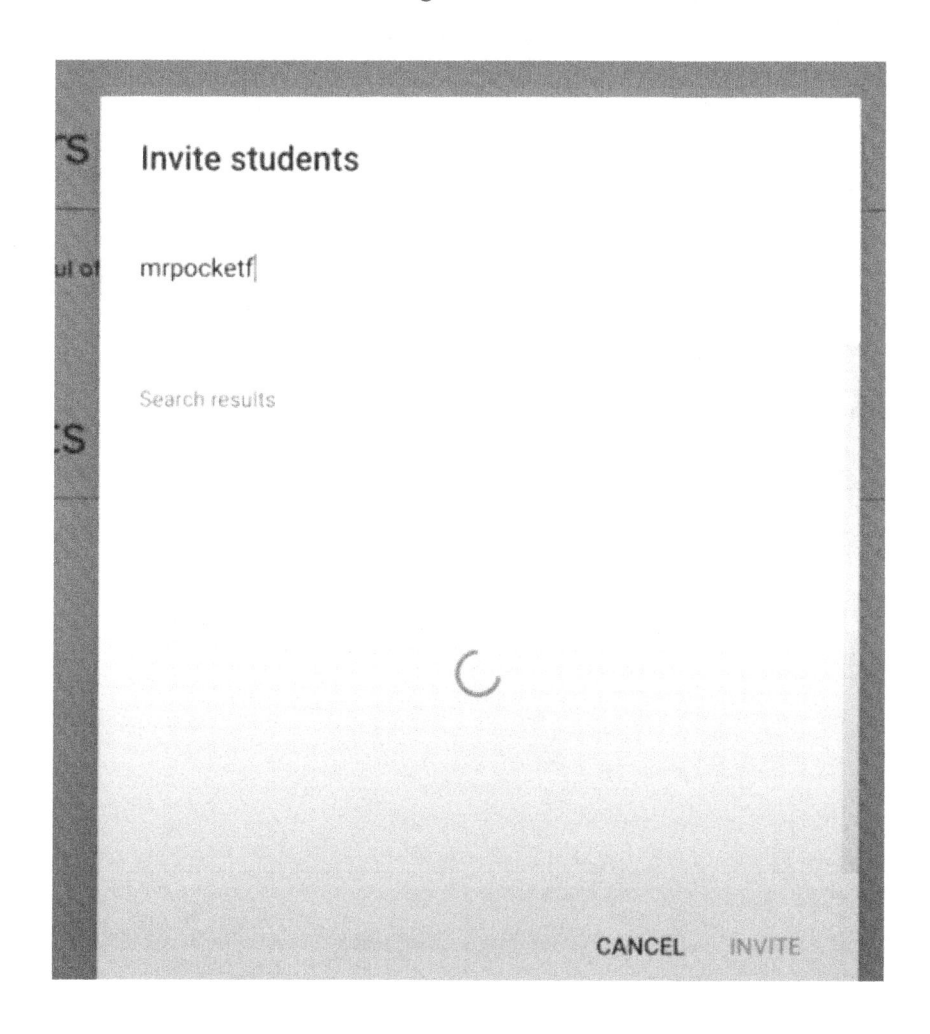

Select students

The first thing to do is to tap on the create control key and select assignment. When you get to the dialogue box of assignment, select the drop-down menu for students and unmark every student and then select the number of students that you want inside the group. If you want to create another group or more, you should repeat the same.

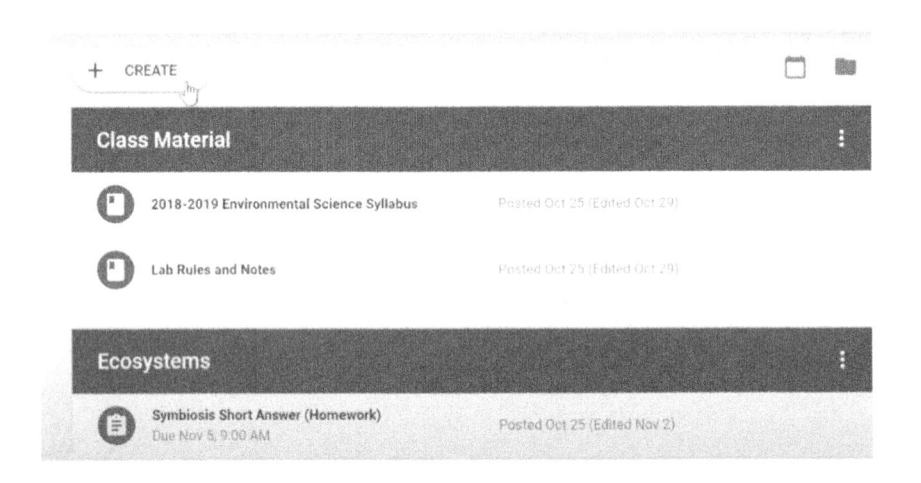

Create homework

Proceed to the dialogue box of homework and find a suitable title for the homework or project which includes the name of the group or additional instructions. Then click on the group task topic, and now you can give the group a task to perform. Now assign the task and ensure that you select, students can edit, in the options instead of creating another copy for every student. Users should make sure that they create a draft for the task before they create the group.

Reuse one assignment for more groups

One exciting feature of the classroom is the reuse attribute which helps teachers a lot. It helps them avoid typing information all over again for each student inside the group. The first thing to do is to select the create control key, then tap reuse post and the dialogue box for the reuse post will display. Click on the post that you want to duplicate and tap reuse. Now you can edit the project as much as you want for the groups. Make sure that you adjust the group members through the drop-down of the student and ensure that you change the number of the group within the controls and title if necessary. Also, you should not forget to remove the homework for a particular group when you want to create a new group. If you do not want to post the homework at the moment of creating the group, you can save it inside the draft folder and utilize it on a later date.

Post group assignments

Whenever you complete the draft of a group assignment, the last step is posting it inside the group so that the students can have access to the project and start working. You will find the draft containing the homework that you create beneath the group topic that you create. Select the three dots menu and tap edit. The conversation box of the homework will show according to what you post, and you should perform the same task whenever you want to post it to groups.

Create a class

The first thing to do is to launch your web application and proceed to classroom.google.com.

What you require to utilize the platform is a Google account, and then you can begin right away.

Select the plus control key to creating a class.

If you are utilizing the platform for the first time, you will have a blank space without any display of previous projects.

If you have previous projects, it will display on the screen, and you can simply tap the plus sign to create a new class which is a faster option.

Add data for the class

The first thing to do is to find a name to make it for easy for users to identify whenever they launch the platform.

Utilize the field segment to distinguish between several classes with similar types. Lots of teachers utilize the field for lots of class projects and period. This is optional.

The subject allows users to select from its lists or input your own.

After creating a class, now add students

Teachers can roll out a code to add to join the class. It is one of the fastest ways to get users into your class because by showing the code, users can sign into the platform easily. Select the plus sign and tap join the class and attach the join code, and you will find yourself inside the class.

Teachers can also get users into the class through the use of email. It is an excellent alternative if you do not hold a physical class that students have to attend in person. To perform this task, select the tab for people on top and tap the invite students control key. Teachers can send direct emails to students or in groups.

Customize the classroom

After creating a class, it will be an empty one, but this is the time where users need to become creative. Tap the select theme, and it will launch the header photos collections where users can add photos to beautify the class.

Users can also upload content to beautify the class, which includes images of a class or anything that looks like a class. A lot of teachers prefer the header image option containing vital information and different graphical images for fun.

Utilize the platform in everyday class

After setting up the class and adding students, the class is now functioning, and students can perform several tasks as well as take instructions from the teachers. But there are few other things that you need to do in the class, and they include:

Add announcements.

This is an excellent way to interact with the class and update them with the most recent information. Teachers post them into the class stream, but it does not associate with the grades. Proceed to the stream and select, share anything with the class. Now users can add text if they want text in the announcement. Users can also include different types of files from the drive or the computer system and then post it or create a schedule for posting at a later date.

Organize topics for the class

Classes can have several units, chapters and objects and if that is the case with your class, you can classify the questions and homework by topic if you want to keep it all organized.

Below the homework, select create button and include a topic for it. Then anytime you create homework or want to announce something to the group, you can add the topic to the content.

Grade projects

Whenever a student completes a project, teachers can give comments and grade the project. Select the class control key and tap the homework to see the project within it.

Below are a few steps to take:

Organize the project by users that submit or by every user handed the project.

Launch and see the student project by selecting it. Teachers can also add a comment directly to the file or input private comments to the projects by selecting the name of the student.

Teachers can now add grades to each student's project.

Now ensure that you check the box with names and select the return control key.

Chapter 4 – How to Set Due Dates, Manage Homework and Assignments

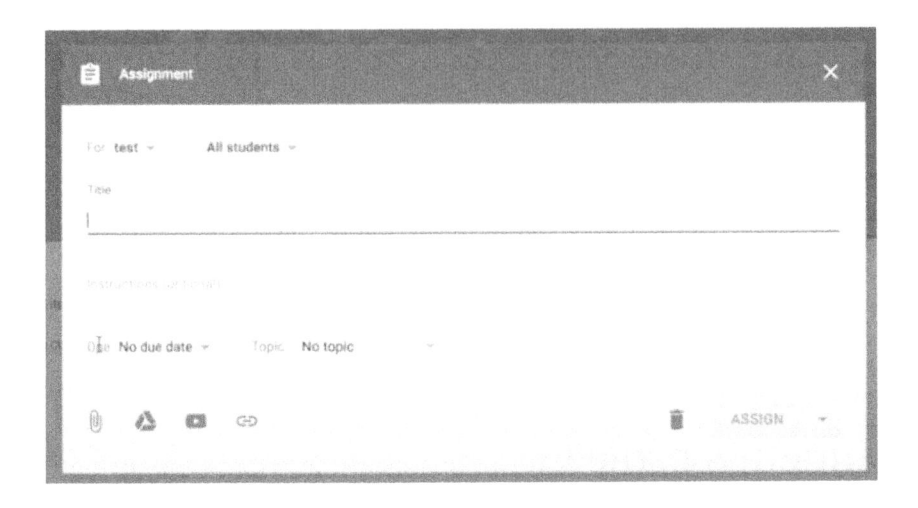

The platform is a digital system created by Google that gives teachers the ability to teach by creating different classes, reply to questions and lots of other tasks. There are lots of different methods for which teachers can utilize the platform and below are few instructions to follow for creating homework and projects for your Smartphones and personal computers.

Create an assignment on the platform

The first thing to do is to log into your Google account and select class.

Hover across the add control key and select generate the assignment.

Input the name of the project as well as its instructions

Modify the project's time or due date

The project will be due the following day, and you should change it to your desired time.

To perform that task, proceed to the segment and select the down arrow

Select the desired date

To set the time, select time and input your desired time

If you want a project without a date, select the due date and tap the remove control key that you find close to the date.

Users can also include different items to the project like audio and video files from the drive, as well as videos from different platforms.

To upload a file…

Click attach

Choose the document and click Upload.

To attach items from a drive like forms and so on, select it and then select add.

Teachers can also determine how users communicate with the item you attached by tapping the down arrow and choosing one of the options where users can view files without altering them, and edit files while altering them. Teachers can also make copies for every student, and they can modify it.

If you want to include a video from YouTube, select add YouTube video and click on one of the available options:

If you need to find the video you want to add:

Select video search

Input the name of the item you are

searching for and select it.

Select add.

To add a video link:

Select the link URL.

Tap add.

To add a link, select the link and input the URL

Select add

If you want to eradicate an attached item

Select remove on the edge of the item

Post assignment into different classes

Select the down arrow that you will find close to the name of the class

Click on the box right after the class you wish to add

Create projects on the platform with Android

Select the classroom and proceed to the class

Click on add and then proceed to the project

Input the name of the class and other important details

Now you can modify the project's time or due date

The project by default will be due the following day, but you can alter it.

Select due date and choose another date and click on the done control key.

Click on time, choose the desired time and select done.

You can include several items with projects such as pictures, videos and so on.

Users can add files by clicking on attach and choosing it

Click upload

Include an item from the drive, select the drive and choose

Click select.

To determine the way users communicate with an included item, select preview and click on one option below:

Edit files and modify it

See the file but cannot modify it

Make another copy for every user, and

each of them will get a one that they can alter.

Eradicate the included item

Whenever you want to add a link, click on it and input the URL

Click on add

To add files, select upload

To add an image, click on the camera and pick your desired picture

Select okay.

To add a video from YouTube, click on attach video

Select one option:

To search for your desired video attachment:

Click on the video search

Input the name and select video

Select add

To add a video link:

Select the URL.

Input it and choose add

To eradicate, tap preview and delete

Distribute the project into different classes

Select add

Choose any extra class and tap complete

Create projects on the platform with iOS

Select the classroom and proceed to class

Click on add and proceed to the project segment

Input the name of the class and additional details

Modify the project time or due date

The project becomes due the following day by default, but you can modify it.

Click on the date and choose another date and select okay

Click on add time and choose a time and select okay.

If you want a project without due dates, you can also remove it

Add items to the project, like links, images, and so on.

Select attach

To add an item from the drive, click on the drive and choose the attachment

Teachers can also determine the way users communicate with the added items by selecting preview and selecting one of the below options:

Users can edit and modify files

Users can see the file, but cannot modify it

Create a duplicate for every user, and they will receive files that they can modify

Users can also eradicate the item

To add a link, select it and input its URL

Click on add

To add a picture, click on pick image or take a shot with the camera and select add

To eradicate an item, select remove.

Chapter 5 – Inviting Students and Teachers to Classes

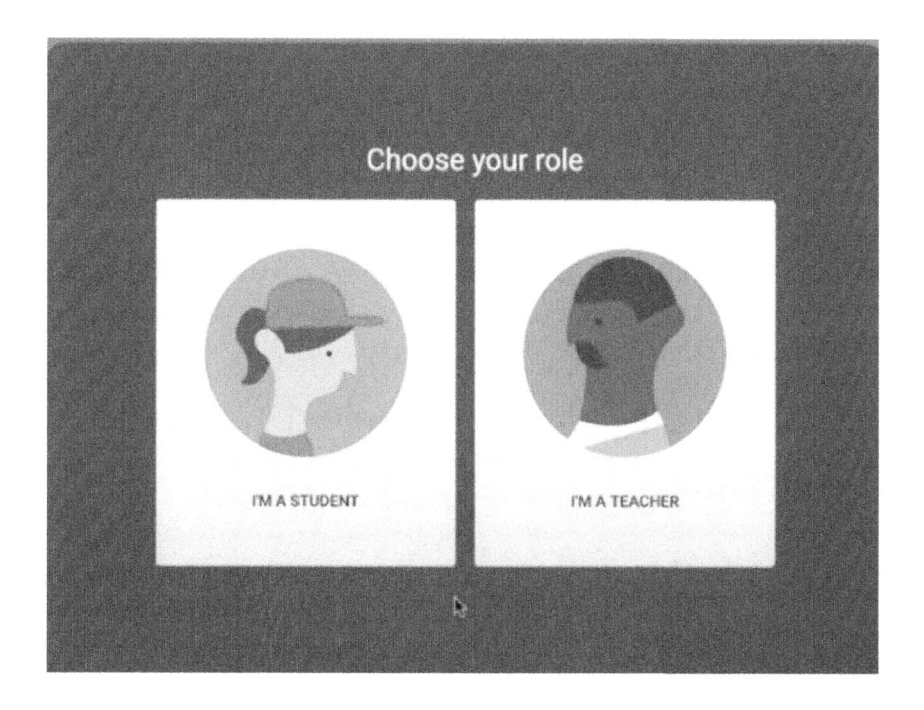

After setting up the class, you need to send requests to students to join the class. Users from the class can get in, or you can also invite them with a code which is one of the easiest methods:

Invite students

Teachers can invite users from the directory of the institution or directly from the teacher's contact or groups. Follow the below steps to perform the task:

Sign in to the class and select the tab for students

Select invite

Within the box for inviting users, tick every box close to the user that you want to invite and select invite students.

There will be an update of the users that joined the class, and the users will get an electronic mail with the class link.

Users should select the link and will get into the class.

Join a class

Before users can join a class, they need to log into the Chrome web browser with the required information. You can get into the class by getting the code from the teacher, and if you are the teacher, you can get students to join the class through the page of the class. Follow the below steps to log into a classroom:

Launch Chrome: The first task to perform is signing into Chrome.

Select the plus sign, and it will create a new tab. It lets users log into the Chrome menu and select the new tab control key.

Log in to the web browser, and it should log you in with the institution's details, but if not, select the name of the person and log in with the email and address with the school account.

Select sign in

Proceed to the platform's official website and click on the enter button

This will redirect users to the page of the class with the join option by selecting the plus logo at the visual display's top.

It will redirect teachers to a page containing lists of the available classes.

If you are utilizing the platform for the first time, click on the Google account when displayed and tap the continue control key. Follow the instructions on the screen to complete the process.

Join the class

If you are a student that shares a computer, then you need to sign the other account out first before you input your login details. Perform this task by selecting the name inside the web browser and tap switch person.

Click on remove a person from the menu that drops down.

Proceed to the classroom's official website and select the plus logo will expand the menu.

Select join, and it will display a box for the code which you should enter and tap join.

You should enter the code the teacher gave you, then the platform will take you directly to the homepage of the class, and you can enjoy the entire process.

If you do not have the code available, you should log into your school email to check for it. Also, get in touch with the teacher as well as other students to know the way forward.

Go through the page of the class because the teacher will leave important information for you on that section.

Users can view upcoming projects in the box that displays on the page left side.

The page will launch the stream tab by default. And that is the collation of posts from your classmates as well as teachers.

Select the project tab at the page's top to check the details of the project.

You will also find the people tab on the right, which shows a list of users. It can be a vital task to perform if you want to reach out to another member of your class.

Select the three-line to launch the menu of the class.

Invite students

Ensure that you log into the appropriate account; you should know that only teachers can invite students into a class.

Proceed to the platform's official website.

Select the class name you want to add

them to. The first thing that will appear when you log onto the platform is your class list.

Select the tab for people

To invite students tap the logo which is the plus sign you will see on the page.

Input the email address of the student; while you type, it will display results that match your input.

Choose the students that you want to include and send them invitations.

They will all receive a code from your class through email. There will be an update on the class after the students join.

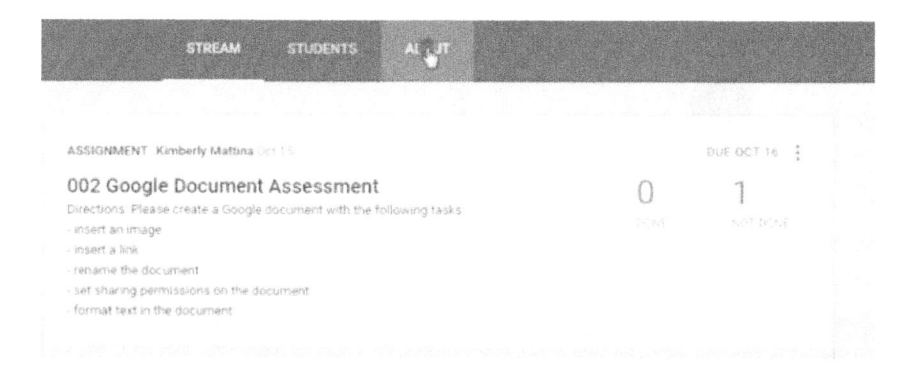

Invite co-teachers

You do not need to be a group owner to add teachers utilizing Google groups. To invite teachers to the groups, you should be able to see the email addresses of members. If you cannot see the list, get in touch with the admin for authorization.

Now proceed to the platform official website and select the class you want fellow teachers to be in.

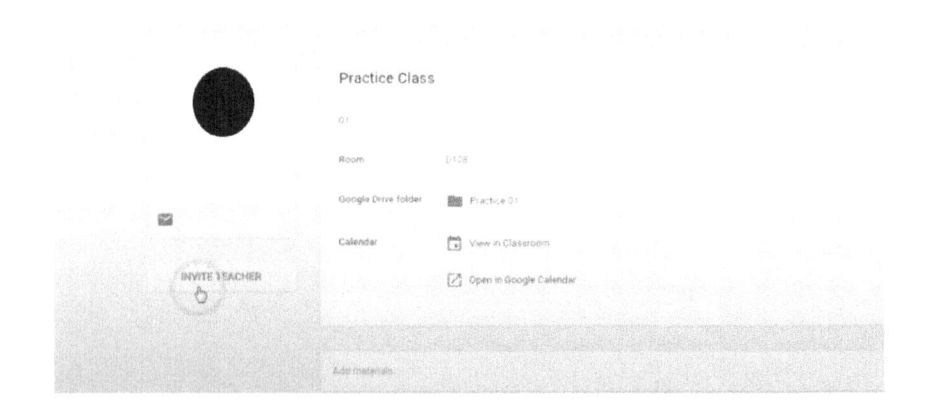

Select people

Tap the invite teachers button

Users can invite teachers individually or in a group. Input the teacher's email address and tap enter

While you input the email, it will display the matching result, and you can choose

Select invite

Teachers will get the invite and decide what to do with it

To join, the teacher will select the link contained inside the email and sign in as a co-teacher.

Chapter 6 – How to Grade Assignments and Then Put Them on Google sheets

The platform ensures that users do not require paper any more for projects and homework. As a teacher, you can create a project or homework for the class with several extra items like worksheets and handouts. Users can now finish a project and submit it right back on the drive. After the students return their homework, teachers can give the projects grades online, and you can perform that with the following steps:

Sign in to the class and select the tab for the stream if you cannot see it on the homepage. Users can find several projects made in that segment

Within the box for homework, see the number of students who have completed the project. And a list of the ones who have not finished will be displayed in that section

Select done, and you will see the number of students who have submitted the project

Select the student's name to enlarge the user's project

To see the content of the project submitted, select the attached document to the project submission. It will launch the file in the right format such as Google docs and so on.

You can insert your comments into the file

There are different styles that teachers can use to write comments on the file, which will be different from the text of the student. It is similar to the olden ways of teachers making comments on students file with a red pen. Also, teachers can utilize the comment tool for feedback. You should perform a highlight on the text that you want to give a comment on and select insert comment. Input the comment and tap okay. Every comment that you make will save automatically inside the submitted document of the students.

Tap exit on the document and go back to the work page for students

Select the no grade button to assign grades to projects

Input your desired points which can be from zero to one hundred. You cannot input letters because it does not have a text field, only numbers

Tick the project box

Select return. You have to return the project to the user before you can record it

The class will ask you to return the project and if you would like to give feedback or comments. After that, you can click the return project button

It will display the project as returned on the list, and the student will get an email update and can modify the project and send it back if required by the teacher.

Any time you create a worksheet for projects, you should utilize the applications from the drive like Google sheets, docs and the likes. This is because the apps have perfect integration with the platform. If you utilize other applications like MS Word, the student will need to download and upload files as well as attach them to the project. The apps from the drives make the process more comfortable and eradicate all the extra work.

Utilize gradebook to improve the platform

This is a platform that lets everyone display and track grades for projects. It also enables the teacher to manage lots of administrative functions on the classroom platform and is one of the important attributes of the platform. It allows an excellent flow of projects, comments and feedback as well as grading, especially when users store the projects on the drive apps such as docs and so on. Teachers can include comments on the Google application, and it also has a sidebar for grading that allows teachers to include a note that the student can read along with the work grade.

Select a grading method

Click on your class and select the sprocket (gear). Proceed to the segment for calculating the grade. There are three methods to select from which are total points, no overall grade and weight by category.

No overall grade means that you will not require a class to track the grades while the remaining two allow the attribute for grading. If you choose the category option, you have to create and input the settings for the category that add a hundred per cent total. If you choose the points option, then you will have to add value to the point of every project. Lots of users utilize the points option because it is easy and straightforward to understand. After selecting the method for scoring, you can create categories for grades and give them values in point or percentage.

Create projects: Select create inside the class tab to include a project, question, or different content. Any time you include classwork, you should choose the category for grades, per cent or point values and also include the due date.

How users complete and submit a project

Whenever users log into the class, they will have access to the project and create as well as finish the project. For instance, as a reply to writing projects, students can create a Google document and can include a link to the new document display on the page for the project. Anytime the user launches the file and edits the document, there will be a turn-in option close to the share button. When the student completes the project, they can submit it in the class, and the teacher will have access to the project and grade accordingly.

How teachers grade and return projects

When a user submits the project, teachers can now include comments, grade the project and return it. The grading view also displays the project for teachers similar to the turn in control key. For instance, whenever the teacher reviews a document submitted by the student, it will display a return control key and a panel that contains a spot for comments. There are some projects that users do out of the system, like activities in class or group communications, and teachers can grade the project manually.

How students and teachers can access grades

On the platform, students and teachers can access the grades for every project. Teachers can also decide if they want students to see the overall grade of the project or not. It is better to let them see the grade and ensure that they know what the score formula is and what it states, if you are sure that you graded them correctly and it is free of errors.

Chapter 7 – How to Motivate Pupils

Motivating pupils can happen in different forms, encouraging them means providing support for people that need it for improvement. Pupils need to know that they have someone they can look up to whenever they make mistakes, who is ready to put them through the process of learning. There are different concepts to use when it comes to encouraging users. Below are a few methods that you can utilize:

Give feedback on projects from time to time. Teachers should give students feedback regularly on each project. It creates a connection between the student and the teacher and in turn motivates the student, which makes it better than individual learning. It improves the student's direction and re-positions their focus.

Whenever a student requires a response, teachers should ensure that they comply within twenty-four hours because it will increase the commitment and focus of the student. Students love to know that someone cares.

Teachers should learn to give constructive comments on projects to create a little source of motivation.

When the students get a low grade, teachers should be another source of encouragement to them and provide supportive feedback.

Draft a message weekly and send to students or post in the class for encouragement, it could be an audio or video messages. Still, it should encourage the students and enable them to get back to learning relentlessly. It shows the student that the teacher is genuinely interested in the learning process and committed to teaching the student.

Ensure that the student knows where to improve. Anytime you want to give challenging feedback, you should point out the student weakness and areas that require improvement.

Be strategic with comments inside the interaction boards. Teachers should be watchful of the comments they make and remarks about users in different student groups and forums.

How the classroom platform helps

You can perform different types of actions with the classroom platform, and this can serve as a source of encouragement to students and help them with their process of learning. Below are a few points where the platform can help students:

Allow students to work together in groups and give them homework

Utilize the Google apps because they make the entire process easy to perform

Give feedback quickly and be encouraging so that students do not get discouraged

Create homework and ensure that they execute them without the use of paper

Create a class and add students

Provide lessons via the application

Share projects and announcements with different classes

Minimize cheating opportunities

Keep track of the projects and know who is not working

Provide flexible hours of work

Give a thorough explanation and example while teaching

New attributes

The platform offers lots of different attributes that can enhance the process of learning for every student, and they include:

Student response

One of the best attributes of the platform is this in-built feature. It gives the users the ability to insert different types of questions into the class page for streams and create an open discussion between students giving replies to each other. For example, users can upload a photo or video and add a question to the caption that the students can answer and discuss. It is also an excellent way for teachers to keep track of students' learning progress quickly and comfortably.

Integrate calendars and re-use assignments

Another important attribute is the ability to re-use an old project or announcement from different classes which saves lots of time when you want to create content similar to the project. It is also advisable to revise the project before you post it. The re-use post attribute helps teachers save lots of time and makes the job easy to perform. You can also sync the platform with the calendar from Google because it places events and projects from the class to the calendar automatically. Users can also see the calendar inside the class. You can also bump a post on the stream to allow users to see it.

You can create projects with no due date for long-term tasks while you attach a form from Google to easily assign surveys and questions to pupils. Of course, the new class technology such as this platform is one of the best but can also produce lots of inconvenience if the wireless cannot support the stream of required devices and what the bandwidth requires. It is best to discuss the wireless network before you connect it to new devices. Ensure that you double-check the network properly.

Interact with guardians and parents

Utilize the class platform to keep parents informed about the student's progress so they can understand the level of the child. You can send an invitation to parents to sign up for a weekly summary of the student or send it to them via email. The message can include the missing works of the student or where the student needs to improve so that parents can be the first teacher of the student.

Utilize Google calendar to organize students

The class platform creates a calendar for every class automatically and provides detailed information about the upcoming projects and due dates. Users can also view dates for tests and any upcoming field events. It is easy to keep track of the calendar, and you should also know that new projects or modified due dates syncs automatically, which means users will see up-to-date information from time to time.

Assign work to a group of students

You can easily assign projects and announce posts to different sets of students as well as individuals inside a class. The attribute lets you distinguish instructions easily and also give support to the users during a group project.

Utilize annotations with the mobile platform application

Teachers and students can utilize the class platform application on Smartphones as well as Chrome mobile gadgets. You can also give appropriate feedback by annotating users' projects inside the application. Students can also annotate projects to express a concept or idea easily.

Integrate the class platform with other tools

The platform utilizes an API to distribute information and connect with different tools. There are lots of applications and websites that you can integrate into the platform, like newsela, peak deck, and so on. You should incorporate any of the applications that the student can relate to easily and use it to teach them, and it will be a source of motivation for them.

Chapter 8 – The Best Google Classroom Extensions

Over recent years, lots of people have pursued a career in digital literacy. It is important to develop the different skills required in this new and advancing world. There are lots of extensions that you can utilize with the class platform to enable easy learning and understanding. Google Chrome provides different types of extensions as well as other institutions, and there are lots that you can use. The extensions from Chrome extends browser functionality and users can use them to get access to important information. Below are a few extensions that you can use to improve your learning and understanding of the platform:

Grammarly

This is advanced equipment for checking grammar and can test your projects for any grammatical errors. The application has a free version that can help users prevent different types of errors when it comes to writing. Another important attribute of this application is that it functions properly on virtually every website, which includes Google mail, docs, and so on. The app also lets users determine the type of English they wish to write, including American and British English. The extended version of the tool also checks for errors and can polish the text from plagiarism. It can provide lots of suggestions on areas that need modification and ensures that you have a suitable text presentation.

Language tool

This is an improved version to the in-built Chrome spellchecker for text mistakes and errors. The tool can also fix any grammatical errors in over twenty different languages. It also functions properly on virtually every website, which includes emails and social media. It underlines the area in a text that requires correction and lets you correct every grammar error with one click.

Save to Google-drive

This gives users the ability to store different types of content to the drive. It also saves time and is a vital tool for students who work a lot with Google applications like drive, docs, and so on.

Store to Google-keep

This functions similarly to the above

option although it's not a popular choice, but one of the best extensions for the platform. You can use the tool to create digital sticky notes that users can utilize to build up lists, include pictures, text, and so on. It also streamlines the entire process by letting users save images and texts from the web by just performing a right-click on the mouse and saving it.

Ginger

It is an excellent application for checking grammar on the web. It gives users the ability to fix an error with one click and also offers suggestions to areas that require fixing and sentences that you need to rephrase. You can also change one line of text by just clicking on it. The tool has a free version that you can use to fix virtually any basic errors grammatically from text from the web. It functions similarly to Google mail, docs and the likes, as well as social media.

Prowritingaid

This is a free tool that you can utilize to check the mistakes on the text and also provides suggestions in areas of the text that requires improvements as well as the text style. The tool can also check your text for plagiarism and functions properly for virtually every website as well as emails and social media. It has an in-built Thesaurus for suggestions on the area that you need to improve. Users can also apply every suggestion with only one click because the tool highlights the text area that you should correct, and when you click, it changes it with the improvement.

Nimbus screenshot

It gives users the ability to capture screenshots and perform a video record by selecting the logo on the toolbar. Users can capture an entire web page or a particular area and then edit the image with several tools for picture editing like text boxes and so on. The tool allows users to record and explain videos on a screen or browser tab.

Google dictionary

This provides definitions of words from the manufacturer's official dictionary. You do not need to copy words to Google to find their meaning anymore, and you can now perform that task by selecting the tool icon and input the word that you want to define. Or double-click on a word in any area of the page and you will see a pop-up box with the meaning of the word you clicked.

Power Thesaurus

It is another free tool that can display the synonyms and antonyms of words on the same page that you can find the word. It will enhance your text and ensures that you can find more suitable words to replace them easily. You can check the tool by clicking on a word and then perform a right-click on the selection. Or select the tool logo and input the words you want to find manually.

Stay focused

If you do not like spending lots of precious time on social media or other unnecessary platforms, this tool is the best for you. It can continue to perform five-minute check-ins whenever you have spent that amount of time on social media. It lets users fix a daily limit of the press and websites that continue to distract you. The tool has a default of just ten minutes, and that is enough time before the tool reminds you. If you are the type that fancies productivity, you should allow the nuclear option through settings and it will block every website. The option can block every site to avoid any distraction and remain focused.

Chapter 9 – Top Five Hidden Features of Google Classroom

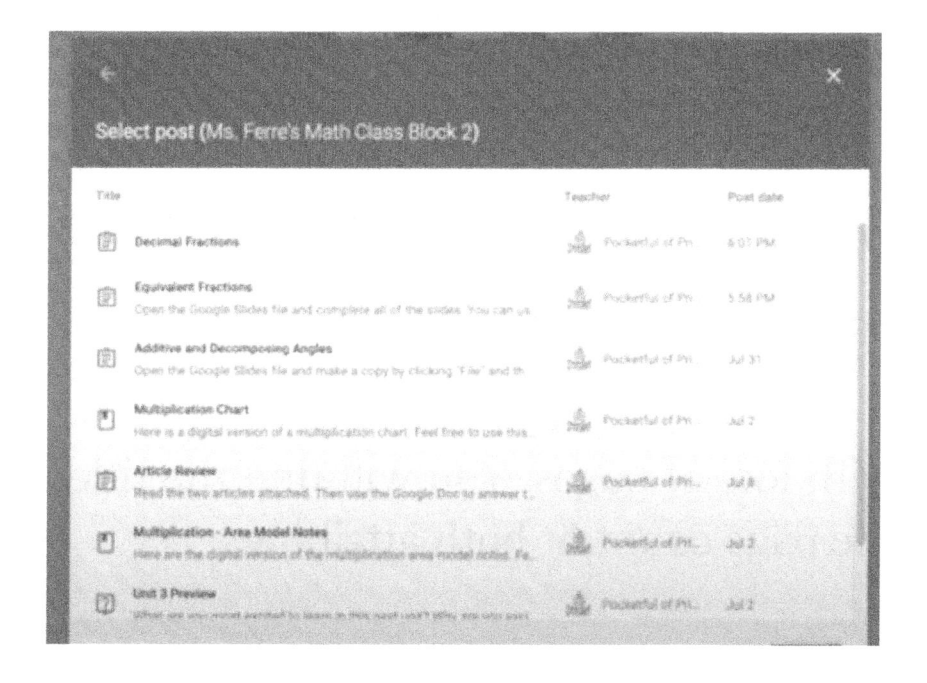

The classroom platform is a popular learning tool for lots of teachers utilizing G Suite because it can blend and function properly with different tools such as docs, sheets and so on. It provides an excellent flow of work for students and teachers by conducting projects and content for the class in a friendly environment. It has lots of hidden benefits that you can utilize in learning surroundings.

Header

It is very integral for building-up a file with lots of pages. You will find the title, the page count or both attributes.

Create

To perform the above task, double-click on one page and input the text. Users can tap the insert key and hover the cursor on the page number and to provide a slide-out that enables the pages to increase in numbers. No matter which method you prefer, you should get a header.

Remove

To perform this task through docs, just take the text inside the header out and perform a click outside the space and then back to the text area. The header will be out of that location.

Change header size

To reduce the size through a file and utilize the field for additional body text, you need to modify the margin. To perform that task, select file and click on page setup. From this location, users can minimize it to the desired size or utilize one pre-set size from the drop-down alternatives. It lets users push and pull it to your desired taste.

Research tool

This is an excellent tool for anyone who engages in writing in docs and to perform lots of research. It lets you perform your research and offers useful suggestions to information relating to the project. It means that you do not have to keep moving from one tab to another.

Users can launch the tool in any of these ways:

Launch the file and proceed to tools menu, then you will see research from the drop-down.

Right-click on any word and tap research

Utilize the control, shift and I shortcut keys.

Anytime you launch the tool, it will display topics similar to your task and you can follow its contributions or not, or utilize keywords. Utilize the menu that drops down if you want to see more information about the topic.

Comments

If you demand lots of answers in class, or you enjoy making notes on existing files, it will greatly improve you. You can attach it directly into the file. It functions similarly to an interaction thread; the more people reply, the more it continues. Anyone can modify or eradicate different comments whenever they want, as well as make contributions on the file. To attach your thoughts in written words, perform a highlight of a picture and tap insert. Select comment from the drop-down, and a field for comment will display.

Tags

If you want your feedback to get somebody's attention, just tag them. You need to include a sign like + and so on and then type your email address or name. Docs provides various options based on your contacts, and whenever you post the comment, it will alert the receiver via email. Sometimes the receiver requires access before they can view the file.

Find and Replace

If you have ever thought of finding different ways to identify an error within your text file, this equipment is the exact solution to that problem. It is an easy tool to utilize on the docs, easier than Microsoft Word. To locate anything in your text file, click on edit and then find and replace from the drop down. Users can also utilize the control and F keys and then tap the three dots on their file. While you are utilizing the tool, if an error displays twice or more, select replace all.

Image editing

Whenever you insert a picture, you still have the opportunity to alter it inside the file. Select the picture inside the file, and you can utilize the toolbar kits to alter the picture. You can add lots of effects to the picture, which includes lights, borders and so on.

Tools for cropping

Click on a picture and select the cropped logo. Now drag and drop the tools until you achieve your desired taste and save it by selecting to enter.

Chapter 10 – Top Useful Apps for Google Classroom

When it comes to the integration of applications, the classroom platform is an excellent team-player for that purpose. It provides an effective and serene place for learning. Users can now integrate lots of applications with the platform, which can make the process of learning comfortable and enjoyable. Installing applications on the platform is a straightforward task to perform, takes little time and functions better and faster. However, there are lots of applications that you can integrate with the platform that users can utilize to distribute information to others individually or in a group. Some of the apps allow users to stream media, build-up presentations and interact with fellow users.

Unicheck

This is a tool that functions excellently with the class platform when it comes to top-quality scanning of your text project. If you are utilizing the platform as a teacher, you can check different students assignments and ensure that the project is an original one and not copied from the web. And if you utilize the platform as a student, it gives you authorship over your projects, and you can defend it easily. One crucial attribute of the tool is that it is different from other tools that you use to check a text for plagiarism because it is for educational projects. The functions that come with the tool work properly for educational projects, and it can easily identify references and citations. The process of integrating the tool with the platform is a simple one, just proceed to the tab where you will integrate it and select Google classroom from the LMSs list.

Discovery education

It is a tool that provides digital streams and textbooks, and videos for several courses like social studies, math, and so on. It can also provide access to different guidelines, professional materials, and so on. The tool offers much more than streaming, it is an excellent choice for learning and makes it much more comfortable because it consists of several components that enhance the process like student assessments and programs, audio clips and lots more. It also enlarges the class information and users can also create engaging content on the tool, which also makes learning more easier.

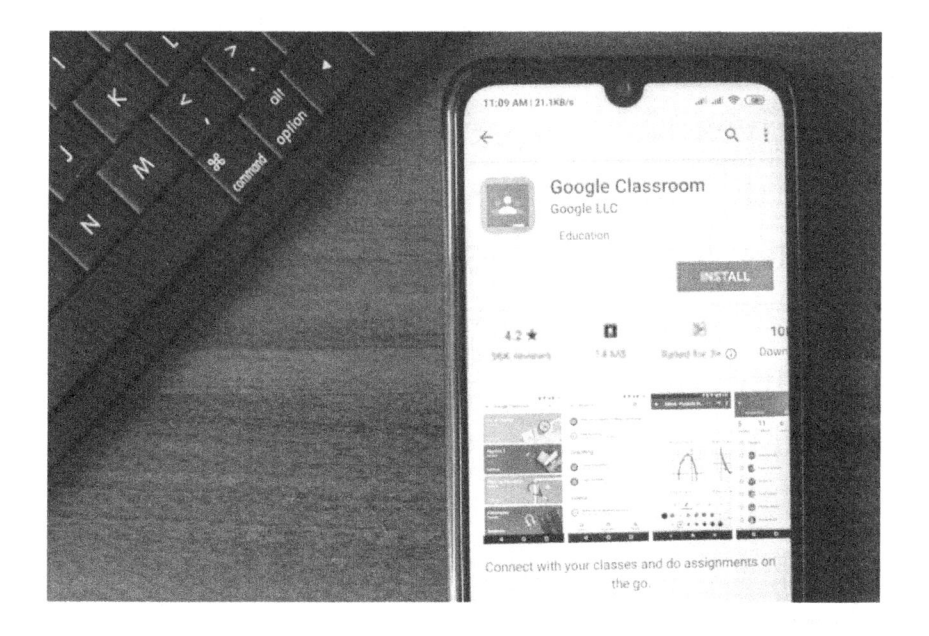

Quizizz

It is a great tool that allows users to teach, create a game for educational purposes, assign homework, and so on, which makes it an excellent tool for learning. It is also a tool that students will love because of its many features. Teachers can create a quiz or utilize the pre-set options from other teachers and distribute them with the class. It is a tool that gives the teacher good control over the students because there are lots of options for teachers to utilize the tool like giving reports and assessments. Teachers can share or assign tasks to lots of students in the same group.

Chalkup

This is a perfect tool for social learning and can help users through lots of tasks like giving homework, grading and interactions. Users can also create personal to-do lists and easily gain access to materials for learning. The tool ensures that grading and distribution of information becomes easier for users with rubric's and also make sure that the grading process is a transparent one.

You can configure the rubric in the table easily, and every class can gain points by submitting projects and then share the points among themselves. It also enhances the interaction between teachers and the students as well as other users.

Duolingo

It is a tool for language learning, and you can integrate it easily on the classroom platform. Lots of institutions utilize the tool and help teachers get comprehensive reports on every student included in a chart. The tool also has a function that allows teachers to track how far every student have gone in the course. It also ensures that users get through several levels without grading and continue to move forward. It offers users the chance to get through different scientific languages tests. The tool has lots of language games to help with the learning process, which makes it fun and exciting.

Zoom

It is an excellent tool that users can utilize in a large group, a large group of students learning or working on a project can utilize the tool even while at home. It is a tool that can create a connection between users and their relatives, friends, teachers and fellow users. It is also an excellent cloud video platform for conferencing that users can utilize for meetings with lots of people. Teachers can utilize the tool to distribute homework, exchange files with students and interact directly with them in a group or individually through the chat inside the app. The tool has a free version for users who enjoy 1-to-1 meetings with a limit time of forty minutes for group meetings. The paid version can perform many more functions than the free version, and it can hold a meeting with at least one hundred participants with a twenty-four hour time limit.

Kahoot

Whenever teaching gets boring, teachers tend to play different types of games to encourage pupils, but there are some teachers without skills from scratch. However, the official website of this tool allows teachers to turn classes into a game zone quickly and easily. The teachers need to store lots of questions and answers on the website to build-up an enjoyable instant game. There are lots of simple tasks to perform that can be fun on the tool's home screen, and users can also check their stats inside the profile section to see how they performed.

Seesaw

This is a tool that gives parents the ability to encourage children during the learning process, and it keeps them in the loop of the kid's performance for the entire school calendar. It is also a tool that can function as a portfolio application for students where they can keep and share their work as well as send to their parents. In addition, it is an excellent tool for teachers to share different exercise examples with students so that they know their strengths and where to improve. It also gives parents the ability to interact with the teacher and hold meetings.

Class tree

Getting pesky forms for parental consent for group field trips can be a problem for students, but this tool ensures that the process of performing that task becomes paperless and straightforward. It also gives notifications of in-coming events and field trips. The tool allows users to include a form for parental consent and to sign the form as well as the announcement electronically. Users can also include extra questions, control feedback and make it easy for students or parents to make urgent queries. The tool also displays the number of people who went through your note, and you get to know who has not signed the form.

Slack

This is an excellent tool for business, and it is also very effective for learning. It is a tool that can keep lots of people together on a network. You can utilize it as a texting tool to stay in touch with loved ones. The tool comes with important reminders that everyone can use through the application. Whenever you want to turn the dark mode switch on or off, proceed to settings and upload lots of pictures one after the other through the box for messages inside the channels.

Trello

Working together in groups can become difficult if every member functions on a separate time. However, this tool ensures that users stay organized; it offers different types of tools that will keep the group focused on the task at hand. It lets users upload pictures, create different checklists, and give homework to students as well as many other actions. It can also easily sync content on different gadgets through the cloud. It displays content inside a layout style of a card-pepper and has options to remove tasks when students complete it. Users can also include different components like links and pictures for quick viewing.

Additio

It is a tool that helps users with keeping notes, grades and attendance easily, unlike other platforms. It is a digital book for grading and controlling the application. You can utilize the tool to calculate students' grades, making your to-do list, and take attendance on your Smartphone. The most recent version of the tool received an upgrade on calculating categories. It also has extra benefits which include keeping notes and so on. There is an advanced version that comes at a price and offers lots of additional benefits.

Dropbox

This is one of the best applications for saving and uploading images for presentations, as well as any item that can be useful for users in a class or while at home and ready to learn. It also allows users to edit and create files for Microsoft offices on Smartphones and distribute documents links to students - not the old way of sending lots of files to the inboxes of students. Users also have control over how other users can access the files through link settings such as passwords when they want to download. It also has enhanced camera parameters which lets users determine which file they want to upload.

Pocket

There are lots of places where people can learn and not necessarily in the classroom, which is one of the importance features of this tool. It offers several ways for saving web content for a future class or an existing one. Users can also see files saved while working on the platform offline, and it displays the document in an easy view layout which makes the reading experience an excellent one no matter your type of Smartphone. It is also very easy to share the articles saved with the rest of the students easily and you can also listen to audio files offline without a network connection.

ClassDojo

This is one of the best tools for teachers to give comments and feedback on students' performances. It gives them the ability to discuss the character of a student with different types of pre-set remarks such as improving, working hard, and so on. It also enables interaction between the teacher and the kid's parent and they can have an input in the progress of their child. Teachers and parents can interact through the private and public mode of messages, no matter the situation of the child's progress. The application does not require a newsletter from schools.

Teacher's assistant-pro

When it comes to organizing projects in the class, you can count on this tool to perform a perfect job. It lets users keep a student behavior record in a class and provides a quick way of identifying bad characters. The tool allows users to see specific email occurrences from the application's interface. It stores information that users enter and keeps the accolade, location and other important events. Teachers can also use the tool to take similar actions, conduct a class and interact with parents as well as many other things.

WolframAlpha

It is a new application that users can integrate easily with the classroom platform. It performs several tasks that includes checking facts, calculating, finding new information and performing different types of research to enhance learning and making teaching easier. It covers a large area of topics and provides information on logical subjects like physics, life sciences, music and lots more. It can also offer help with subjects such as finance, geography and the likes. It is equipment important for everyone and does not leave out students or teachers.

Groovy Grader

If you are the type of teacher that still gives grades the old way, then this tool is for you. It helps users improve and updates your calculating ability of students' grades. The tool takes the place of a paper grading calculator and is more flexible in finding out the precise and fair grade to award a student. Users can also configure the application for lots of questions and ensure that it shows the grades in whole numbers or decimal places. You can use the app to check correct and incorrect grades and has an excellent combination of colour-coding. Users can see more than fifty grades at once on the visual display.

Educreations

This is a tool that allows users to create straightforward tutorials for learning and is easy to integrate into the classroom platform for educational purposes. Users can create audio records to discuss events, and it lets you make commentary and give comments as well as animations on any topic of your choice. Users can also distribute different types of content with each other, which includes email and social media. The most recent version of the tool can provide access to your saved drafts across all devices.

Conclusion

This book contains much vital information about Google classroom. The concepts here give users a good understanding and excellent usage of the classroom platform. It starts with an introduction to Google classroom, and everything about it. How to begin with the tool, its benefits for the general public, how to manage and create a class, setting up dates and managing assignments and homework, grading homework and placing them on Google sheets and so on. You will get explanations on how to invite teachers and students to class and lots more.

I hope, that you really enjoyed reading my book.

Thanks for buying the book anyway!

Made in the USA
Coppell, TX
28 August 2020